PRAISE FOR ADRIAN ERNESTO CEPEDA

Adrian Ernesto Cepeda's sensual, electric internal rhythms provoke external, communal ones too. And La Belle Ajar is not just an exercise in homage but a choreographed remix, a translation, a correspondence between words and worlds. Cepeda leaves the door open, in pursuit of readerly access and inspiration. This work vibrates.

CHRIS CAMPANIONI,
EDITOR PANK MAGAZINE
AND AUTHOR OF *THE
INTERNET IS FOR REAL*

Adrian Ernesto Cepeda's *La Belle Ajar* is delightful, thought-provoking, and compelling. The lines are both conversational and fierce, lulling us into submission, and then chilling us to the bone at the same time: "she burst /out, I never said, I'm not/godlike." Cepeda takes Plath, and digs in deep to her life, her struggles, her being, while inhabiting the world as it is now, while conveying the very strangeness of being at all: "I looked empty and subdued,/among the Gillett blades/paper scraps it occurred to/me, I must be idly dead." This book is meant to be read and loved, with all its complexities, much like a human."

JOANNA C. VALENTE, AUTHOR OF *MARYS OF THE SEA*, #SURVIVOR, AND EDITOR OF *A SHADOW MAP: WRITING BY SURVIVORS OF SEXUAL ASSAULT*

Adrian Ernesto Cepeda's new book *La Belle Ajar* opens up Sylvia Plath's words and gives them new life, ballooning up inside and splitting the reader between memories of *The Bell Jar* and a look inside the eyes of Cepeda's reborn character who 'looked at half-dark desire' embracing an edgy, sexy vibe. This fresh discovery into each chapter of Plath's novel is delightful, delicate, and consuming. With 'eyes dancing water-color / firecrackers' and 'thick lips, dirty-minded skin', you'll fall in love with this new rendition of womanhood, desire, and seeing a woman come alive as she 'began to thrive soft curiosity / flickering alive, flutteringly / loved in the dark garden heart / of New York.'

TIANNA G. HANSEN,
EDITOR-IN-CHIEF OF
RHYTHM & BONES PRESS

How often are we able to reread Sylvia Plath's words as new poems? In *La Belle Ajar,* Adrian Ernesto Cepeda succeeds in the challenge of bringing lines from each chapter of *The Bell Jar* into our current world. These poems inspire with Plath's vitality and Cepeda's careful crafting. Cepeda finds the magic of Plath and delicately constructs her enchantment into these breathless poems which delight with energy. *La Belle Ajar* is a beautiful collaboration between the dead and the living, the muse and the inspired, and a reminder to continue the conversations with the poets who came before us.

KELLI RUSSELL AGODON,
EDITOR AT TWO SYLVIAS
PRESS AND AUTHOR
OF *DIALOGUES WITH
RISING TIDES* (COPPER
CANYON PRESS)

In *La Belle Ajar*, Adrian Ernesto Cepeda has the philosopher's stone. He changes Plath's already-gold prose into 24-karat verse with a sleight of hand known only to the world's greatest seers and fire-stealers. Cepeda does Plath justice here, in her own words, and accomplishes his goal of creating a companion piece to the novel in poems that crackle, pulverize, and shimmer.

KIM VODICKA, AUTHOR OF
THE ELVIS MACHINE

A sensuous meditation on Plath's masterpiece, which reads as smooth as honey. Cepeda summons Plath's spirit, which beautifully haunts every page.

ANNA SUAREZ, AUTHOR OF
*PAPI DOESN'T LOVE ME
NO MORE*

Plath's eternal essence — her poetry of confessions, rife with details and darknesses — is woven throughout this La Belle Ajar. The drama, the particulars, and an unlimited glimmering of language oozes in each and every poem. The ghost of Plath seems to be conjured, to find reanimation, in Cepeda's many inspirations. And while Plath is the muse here, of course, the work stands entirely on its own — unexpected, surreal, and alight. A true tribute, emerging into its own new shape.

LISA MARIE BASILE, POET,
EDITOR OF LUNA LUNA,
AND AUTHOR OF *THE
MAGICAL WRITING
GRIMOIRE*

LA BELLE AJAR

CENTO POEMS FROM SYLVIA
PLATH'S 1963 NOVEL

ADRIAN ERNESTO CEPEDA

CL4SH

Copyright © 2020 by Adrian Ernesto Cepeda

ISBN: 978-1-944866-66-2

Cover by Matthew Revert

matthewrevertdesign.com

CLASH Books

clashbooks.com

La Belle Ajar is dedicated to Sylvia Plath and the next generation of writers and poets who are inspired by her timeless words and volumes of fiction and poetry. We need a generation of Plaths to spark young writers to carry on the torch that was lit in such classics as Ariel, The Colossus, The Bell Jar and the rest of her canon of works that are waiting to be read, reexperienced and rediscovered by the next poet

... I am hoping she is you.

Though lines get repeated, and sometimes the plot is lost, language never dies in her mouth.

- **ROBERT LOWELL** ON **SYLVIA PLATH**

I write only because
There is a voice within me
That will not be still

— **Sylvia Plath**

PREFACE

Sylvia Plath's poetry has been inspiring me for years. Recently, her words, specifically, her letters, diaries, short-stories and prose — have been speaking to me, creatively. After rediscovering a copy of *The Bell Jar* on our bookshelf, I decided to try to craft a cento poem. A cento is a poem composed of lines from another source. In this case, I was so enchanted by Plath's words that I went through each chapter and attempted to honor her by crafting cento poems from the words in her book. Each chapter I discovered in *The Bell Jar* was a new challenge and opened possibilities. Creating this chapbook, of twenty poems, one for each chapter in *The Bell Jar* has been one of the most exhilaratingly challenging projects of my career. *La Belle Ajar* is an homage to one of my favorite poets. When people ask me why: my goal for this project is to hopefully inspire younger poets and writers to experience the timeless artistry that is Sylvia Plath. If I can spark one reader to dive into the literary world of this American literary legend, then this ambitiously colossal chapbook will be worth this creative journey. Long Live Sylvia Plath.

Thank you for the inspiration, Sylvia!

1

THE SUMMER OF GOGGLE-EYED HEAD

Lines, fake country wet
freshness, blew into
my eyes like some black
noiseless balloon, I was
supposed to be drinking
martinis, having a real
whirl. Look, I wasn't
steering, there was twelve
of us in the same little gilt
box. We kept the starfish
off the sunglasses, hard
and polished. It suggested

a whole life of fake eyelashes
in bed with the smart girl,
tears in her eyes, smiling.
I could hear everything she
said. I liked feeling almost
naked. I sat tight, their eyes
fiddling blasé, edging ahead
my hips in a sideshow, dogging
along, she looked silver full
of vodka, my dream wasn't
saying a word, I wanted
her mouth, a high silly

voice, pickled all the time
giving me a wink, she burst
out, I never said, I'm not
godlike.

2

IN THE SHAPE OF A
HORSESHOE

She was relieved, stiff
jackrabbit ears sunflower
funny, crossed-legged
against the wall, she giggled
like sweat lingered. My drink
was wet, another sip
of an express caboose
kiss, whirling around her
teeth stooped, swinging melons
leaning then sucking up
Doreen's breasts, under
my breath, glittering so

perfectly crawling dirty
in love till the holy baptism
bathtub pink marble jazz
waters, pool of concrete
dissolving liquor kisses,
hot purer, tap-tap, dizzily
blinked out mustached woman,
listen to heat hearing her spiked
heels moan, sunless resembled
my face a pile of pillows, she
leaned even heavier lipstick,
quietly loyal at heart—her

vomit wisps hissing too heavy
hiccups already she's half-asleep.

3

I WAS STARVING

I love food with one exception
I splatter, dripping appreciation
for passionate chicken fingers,
hidden dressing tasted salty
licked thick lips, a scalding beauty,
lying in my room, tempted, hungry
why don't you come? My eardrums
ringing as he spoke wilderness
into the sheets, hanging manic
depressive, his affairs
were quite scalding. He burst
bustling grapefruit juice excited

with a double-barreled sex cycle,
he grooved making blue flames,
his colored fires sparked
appreciative smiles, he made me
dizzy—a sweet little ingenious
glance, quite flattered—I couldn't
help pretending to be touched
by Shakespeare.

MY SUCCESSFUL EVASION
OF CHEMISTRY

All the time I saw
the pink lady her gilt
trumpets lips. I secretly
dabbled, between the table,
my fingers carefully bloomed
like a tiny heart still alive embossed
in suspenseful questions, secluded
bleak her moonlit pillows, where
I saw cherry blossoms and I ate
every bit of a fingerbowl debutante.
I learned in the warm throbbing
cave, red hair, sexy technicolor

chrysanthemums into the nasty
smart mistress—I looked at
half-dark desire, ballooning
cheeks driving light as her bathrobe
waves undressed on the floor.
I sat limp glittering my head
in pieces, I stretched my bones,
they kept banging flushed
as molasses. My eyes swam
comforting voices and groans,
to the chin, fanning one plump
withholding sympathy, I drifted

pillow cracked and my nose
contemplated the shadow tenderness,
of a windowsill cigarette, ptomaine
against infinity, her expert fingers
seductively finally seeing—her
name a mouthful she came, Doreen—
echoed in my lap stretching
our sound in the holy mirror.

AT SEVEN, THE NEXT
MORNING

Slowly I swam, reached out
onto my pillow, my collarbone
detected hands. He was
ugly, a touch for a bite,
stiffly, laden with special meaning,
feeling passionately grim,
I looked down, he came—
First, like a hypocrite he was
beautiful by accident, I could
go down, asked for cold taps
in my washbowl, switching
the hot and the cold, uneasy,

I kept insinuating curious about
his tip. Perfectly, I let him, flourish
a little, smile by mistake, I think
I opened the bed-jacket, inside
lying down, asleep—I came,
hatching, touched hands
together, mean faced, a lovely
story, as I lay there, I wanted
to crawl, I felt like a heel, dust,
I just stared fig teeth and blue
eyes, I guess I finally could, smiling
cadavers are curing. I couldn't

repeat, remember he kissed me,
it was strange between us,
his handsome sweater staring
flabbergasted blister, surprised
pale, mushroomy grinning up,
eyeing me curiously, oh come,
I said. I went cold, gleaming
in there. My floor started speaking
dull and flat, our mouths
shattered hastily, my hand
pretending, tell everybody
I imagined almost hot—

I wanted to memorize
his uninspiring kiss.

THE ARROW SHOOTS FROM
INFINITE SECURITY

My eyes peered unpleasant
thinking it must be an insult—
somebody stood thin, I noticed
a dark shaven fuzzy thing
between her head. I heard
no makeup, waxy skin
uncorked wine of regret. Trying
to introduce me naked, hinting
around to stay clean, how fine
I felt my nylon fishnet
practically engaged, I stood
staring undressing his turkey

neck. Naked, hair down,
an affair of my virgin mouth.
I rhythmically could feel
my hot cheeks clinging sexy,
petting my cheek, every stroke
seduced confusion, I was
the future, in the eye something
froze. My pleasure breasts admit
to sleeping with another boy,
nothing between us, so pure,
sexy— broken perfect all over,
I couldn't breathe, laughing

about his virginity.

HANDSOME IN HIS
OWN WAY

With an American tan and such
good intuition, we cracked a
a dry eyebrow laugh and pretty
languages, happier with no make
up eyes dancing water-color
firecrackers, ideas rattling
off lively, challenging expressions
and I wished I could crawl and
spend breakfast stranded like water,
I wanted to be shrunk like a garlic
salt dancer, glory upon his mantel,
I winked, I wanted wrinkled lovers,

very clean, three-dimensional lace,
I floated, flushed smoke-dark flame
like I withered an empty stomach,
he kept refilling coffee, sweet
strawberry sex jam, we drank
necking madly, a Biblical cup
thick lips, dirty-minded skin,
love me seduced, my balalaika
baby, I felt tender, one hundred
percent moved, two worlds
pure, red-blooded pickle sex
a spectacular hour, street lights

like stars, drifting drunk, I said,
casually, I'll go down, nudge
off my sigh, lying my hands
glimmered under his beautiful
tan skin. I wanted excitement,
he came shapely bone, flawless
he moved the sound of pitch
black rain closer, outlines
of air, the sound of my breath
lifted up, my eyes grew darkness,
I leaned over, my nightgown dirty
he was utterly big, we clicked,

his tip quite still, l lay in bed,
he needed my lace, my ache
would rouse me, peaceful
fingers, cheerful I came
fumbling the blur of tenderness
breathing exhausted, I stared
at his electric eyelids.

8

IT WAS THE DAY AFTER
CHRISTMAS

I was crying last crumbs
of grey air, rosy-cheeked
eyes thick mountain lungs
Tuna fish throat, dark
glowering malady, I felt
disappointed stains my dark
face bitten veneer, sun
drowse sputtering mottled
hands, fleshless cheekbones
sounded smiling moist
and fat, liver-colored odor
bruised Lilly pad breathed,

I grew gloomier with a silver
hair expression, I was surprised
comfortable birch-log fires, smoke,
thin, dull of fir tree sickness,
I hesitate gray like bits of extremely
sinister aura, his boring look,
my unpromising eyes, old falls
silver snow vision of a small
voice, my whisper eye adoring
a distance, stiffly brightened
the perfect neurotic night
dimmed, thinking the worst

voice, scornful gesture, all
morning persuading his one
size anatomy, my pupils numb,
let's try a zigzag momentum,
hands slithered behind me,
he hung poised, open my bright
throat blurred, focusing my skin
like a flower mosquito, descending
horizontal, my own body secrecy,
smiles receded unfastening
a familiar man inched
up probing, strokes,

like a distracted wand
I wanted a smooth sweet
weapon, edging straight
down, dispassionate mouthful,
my throat expression, a final
smile came... crushed.

9

I'M SO GLAD THEY'RE
GOING TO DIE

Like a tropical bird,
a wisp of her arms
arched, kissing my brain,
I cursed the frosted heroine,
her voice sounded sick
in an electrocuted reflection.
I waited in morning gloom,
Her orange mouth yawned,
two lips possessed, amplified
and met. Sloshing and brimming,
we wanted eyes too closely
facing, concealing her hands,

my face unsteady, a paper
rose picture. The frieze
of hot white cloud lights,
puffs traveling obediently,
my mouth prowling of sight,
it's paws the gift of mascara,
I breezed back, peering puffy
and bruised, where you sent
me a gift of nylons, lipsticks,
magnificence might rub me off,
all grubby, underwear spread
beautiful and perplexed, stockings

snowballing into the bed, finally
dazzled hard hand the spark
matching the gold knob,
reminded me of a breathing
diamond snake. The stout
opened to rattle a smile.
My hand reached dazzling
odors of cool flowers and
riveted single cricket music,
I breathed out vaporous light,
ghost pale of love his mouth
unreal to touch her, my fingers

squirmed, it hissed at his leg,
like a link I sucked the darkness,
of salty knuckles, his enveloping
fingers perfectly grasped
my breast, I waved truce,
my own hunt spun around
between the refugee's suburbs
I began to thrive soft curiosity
flickering alive, flutteringly
loved in the dark garden heart
of New York.

10

WHAT A HOPSCOTCH THE
WORLD WAS!

I glanced at the wings
of my blouse, I ghosted
swarming over New York
with a lampshade
and my bathrobe. I smiled
my face of a dead lover,
blood disturbing my lips
a little avocado thunder
cannoned the breath
of a spectacular picture
I spoke Italian through
my domesticated wilderness,

as a slippery and lovey hand
soothing my spine. I filtered
sulphurous light into exhaustion
of clothes, the soprano
squeaked, kissing my naked
stomach, I tilted an unsociable
gaze, my zombie ass, never living,
choose the sweat of a mattress
impression. Tombstone like,
I squinted untranslatable voices,
my brain embarrassing dead keen
with an intuitive glittering touch

I could see the squinted dark eyes
reflection, my strange lover study
the freckled marshmallow tenderness
of my Pollyanna Cowgirl throat
my face lit up a religious smile
like a nervous trilled bird
raw with infatuation.

11

AT FIRST, I WONDERED
WHY THE ROOM FELT
SO SAFE

The walls were pale green,
the darker mirrors made me
shiver. I hadn't washed
my sweaty sour hair
for seven nights, I must
have slept, my green
friendly eyes wide open,
like black shade the white
clock seemed silly, I twiddled
an imagined man, so scared
I would match his fingers,
so perfect his smiling features,

I turned the wrong conceited
words over, I made a tired sound,
I had a dull flat beguiled voice,
I tried haloing a string of cleverness,
revealing my slim shoulder
unkindly praying, with a hastily
reminiscent smile, I remember
suspiciously hiding in little pieces,
one move, peering up, beside me
the inner walls were dun-colored
unconventional I would love a
tender sailor, his white G.I.

cupcake hat, I suggestively attracted
the longest stare. The sailor
quickly squeezed a kiss, I was
only asking to make out, hands
across my cheek, his little hot
chin quivered unimpressed,
I cracked open my eyes, he
had something tiny on his smudgy
face. He saw my breasts wiggle
imagine as his mouth tasted
naked balloons. My upper
crescent skin, crackled a hot

dusty static word, his hands
happened to feel my encouraging
"ah!" in one smooth lean back
semicircle virile move his loud
face grinned subway directions,
I felt his surging sandy-mouthed
courage— swallow me all night.

12

THE SOUND OF THE CICADA
ONLY SERVED TO
UNDERLINE THE
ENORMOUS SILENCE

I approached the crazy
people, bothered
in the heart, I knew
I could see normal
and no wild noises,
the lopsided grand piano
sweetened the sunlight,
without speaking I focused
on birdlike gestures,
my gaze stirred speaking
to shock treatment faces,
my eyes peered out

with thick spectacles
I leaned like a cloud
my smile had gone stiff
I saw a keyhole of death.
I bent down crackling
the end of the world stench
the lamp rattled me upside
down, stuck, I tried to scream
my hands splayed, my knuckles
thumbed a slow almost tropical
music smile. With dead spit,
I lingered pantherlike, my mind

pirouetted the snapshot into
a chrome large shadow space,
my flesh winced, I felt
a second wave of death sitting
collapsed, the drench cold
under my bare feet, I could
sense worried, I thought
of razors pointing, I said
good-bye, I could feel
red tears like a guillotine
my shadow paralyzed,
circling my ash-colored head,

I looked empty and subdued,
among the Gillett blades
paper scraps it occurred to
me, I must be idly dead.

13

OF COURSE, HIS MOTHER
KILLED HIM

I looked at his lips, thick
and pink mouth California
baby face, I wondered if he
was cute, his white-blonde
hair soft looking fire on
the sand, my mind swimming
beach burned, I squinted bright
stony old-fashioned haze,
perfectly I rolled with make
-out eyes welcoming a clear
glassy skyline. He had gills,
underneath, his head treaded

water, I would swim dull
motor heartbeat, panting
heavily I boomed shadow less
light. Out there, my eyes
seared, I am myself, I am
hanged, poor knots, longing
my neck to fasten and silk
chord dangle my face a flush
of mother's blood. My body
limp, my tongue hopeless
scandal. I remembered the day
after my hanging fiasco,

I watched like a white sea
worm, my pointless head
dived, sparkling a yellow lie
to myself. My eyes dashed,
panting, I dived with a word,
pushing three flights, the grimy
elevator felt cold as a hospital
morgue pushing gruesome
echoed floating like a semi-
precious tomb. With a sharp,
jazzy voice, I stuffed giggles
in the middle of the room.

Vases of dead flowers bowed
to me. I didn't believe
in an infallibility graveyard,
I could just concentrate on
hearing the virgin priest's feet,
funny, yearning for a black-veil
funeral, I imagined killing myself.

14

I FELT DARKNESS, BUT
NOTHING ELSE

I felt like the head
of a worm, moaning
the weight of stopped
darkness. Rumbling
transported, disagreeing
with silence, the voices
cracked back, a wound
wrapped like a slit round
my mouth. The chisel air
struck my body, I felt a hand
bending shapes on my face.
His fingers floated and perfectly

I arched like a silver hair
exotic bird and plunge
sandwiched I sat between
the blue-sky closed eyes
under the glass stewing
bell jar. I heard voices
hummed, my wing, perfectly
untouched, grateful the inner
bell I hadn't heard the stir,
of subtle air inside the window
jar, quietly let out a tiny toy
box sounded like an ordinary

size hell. I liked the flashes
of smoke. The noise. My skin
jolting. First came the smell.
Matches made of intense candy.
I disappeared without looking,
I didn't speak, my silk pajamas,
glanced back, my buttocks purple
scars savoring the hurt from asylum
injections. I laughed, appreciating
my improbably postcard escape,
a telegrammed mistake, never
leaving, I was marble angry,

an untouched lobotomy
without a stream of thinking.
Always gleaming confusion,
I enjoyed my unmistakable lapse
into speechless treatments,
overcooked to shock me, emptying
the breath of my cheerful disbelief.
probed and disappeared,
my flabbily skin quivered,
I covered my legs, laughing
a crazy stripped mirror memory,
arms folded, I listened funneling

my mother's artificial superstition.
Suspicious, I looked and gawped
at crazy eyes people. Scattered
naughtiness, my fingers began
to crack, a million little shards,
I couldn't imagine the mirror,
my skin trembled in the corner,
grating, I always saw I tried to kill,
my ugly body, starving solemn
I tightened my mouth, stiff
feeling, huddled inside myself,
my tongue stuck, I smiled a

shapeless secret—I pretended
I wanted to be nobody.

15

ONE JUMP AND THE WATER
WOULD BE OVER MY HEAD

I arched like a silver hair
exotic bird and plunge
sandwiched I sat between
the blue-sky closed eyes
under the glass stewing
bell jar. I heard voices
hummed, my wing, perfectly
untouched, grateful the inner
bell I hadn't heard the stir,
of subtle air inside the window
jar, quietly let out a tiny toy
box sounded like an ordinary

size hell. I liked the flashes
of smoke. The noise. My skin
jolting. First came the smell.
Matches made of intense candy.
I disappeared without looking,
I didn't speak, my silk pajamas,
glanced back, my buttocks purple
scars savoring the hurt from asylum
injections. I laughed, appreciating
my improbably postcard escape,
a telegrammed mistake, never
leaving, I was marble angry,

an untouched lobotomy
without a stream of thinking.
Always gleaming confusion,
I enjoyed my unmistakable lapse
into speechless treatments,
overcooked to shock me, emptying
the breath of my cheerful disbelief.

16

HOW DID YOU GET HERE?

I was engaged hearing
my own twisted image,
hidden blood-red humoring
the terrible mirror I had
awakened a crazy smile,
black-shadowed lips, awful
eyes glinting white flesh,
I looked puckered quiet, faint,
like a dim yellow flame cigarette,
I could hardly explain
to my sorrowful mother
why it occurred to me to kill

myself. Begging me to chat,
my telephone buzzer sounded
hurt, my life utterly confounded,
satisfied with tasting luxurious death
I braced my tongue to disappear.

17

YOU'RE A LUCKY GIRL
TODAY

Like a passenger
moving on the sea air
I'm not ready, breakfast
hadn't changed. I heard
beaming, the gulf between
me and shock danger, quiet
and extinguished I sat
like a little doll, listening
quietly the panic in my head
sounded like piano music
my tongue full of dread
told me to rim a lid on nasty

debutantes talk, avoiding
my mouth awake encouraging
my heaviness to squeeze
a strapless breath, soft
on the back of my burnt-out
neck. The nights groaned,
I'm frozen, I woke up with
a stir of pleasure, mouth opened
love speaking in a confidential
tone, howling tangled, full of
forbidding dread, electrotherapy
surprised me like death. Protruding

through the craters of my eyes,
I bit down smiled at the machine
"Promise you'll strike me dead"
Surprised I was when the hissing
darkness bent and wiped me
on both sides of my savage bed.

18

I WOKE OUT OF A DEEP DRENCHED SLEEP

I saw my bell jar hung
awkward blue-skied air
purged with fear, suspended
heat, shock silver cracked
breathless noose on this
bird my spine grinned
like an empty air fruit fly
I waved to the wonderful
creeps in hell. Hearing
no half-useless answer,
my vision ached, I never
really liked my puke fingers,

mocking a little fascinated
shape of a smile, I hesitated,
devoting the next step to
embracing my own virgin
voice, under this disappointed
nose, eyes fixed, bending
transparent full and unnoticed,
my own black image cried,
I just wanted the music turned
on mingling nasty pink fuzzy
songs with the extinguished
gloom in my mad sex expression.

19

I'M GOING TO LIVE
OUT NOW

My mind saw polar
chills, I spoke shrewd,
breathy chattered, I was
hurt. My envy abstract,
I decided to ruefully
seduce a bosomy smile—
his wistful enthusiasm
bespectacled and promising
my vivid lips drank his hairless
virginity, he unsettled,
engaging in modest ugly
ice-encrusted hesitations,

sipping, I demanded a load
of his dirty tribal wine juice,
my mouth drank his enormous
paradise confession, naked
as white smoke, he admired
the warm between my legs
seepage, his fingers began
to probe, oozing with a grin
wide-eyed, blinking, my outlines
rustling at attention, I pushed
him to journey into a little death,
my mouth opened every beat

immaculate, my midnight pulse
climbed and released another
rigid flush—he leaned back. riding
me, my dark face smiled spectacular.

20

SUNK IN A MARBLE CALM

Christmas snow blanketed
me, my eyes saw a flicker
of strangeness: am I, I am,
am I...I was grateful
the envious bell jar dreamed
of ice, pure snowflakey sky
martyrs. My confused gray
skull sunk shivering suicides.
My shadow adrift of revenge
eyeing a black ground cadaverous
underfoot funeral. I saw my nervous
labyrinth wound stuck rising knee

deep in tombstones, a candlelit
gesture touched me smiling
impatient, I followed as my eyes
stepped over faces of white masks,
no longer scared of death, I waited
burying eye batting question marks—
glances, my coffin departure
would be the last cry. So long
shoveled grave emotion stinging
of bell jars. Drained of listening
to kerchiefed spinterish boredom—
my relived breath creaked good-bye.

AFTERWORD: COMMUNING WITH SIVVY

OR HOW SYLVIA PLATH SAVED BY INSPIRING ME TO CRAFT CENTO POEMS FROM HER NOVEL THE BELL JAR

EVERY NIGHT, SINCE I FINISHED *LA Belle Jar,* I commune with Sylvia Plath. I call it going to Plath school, learning everything I can about the poet/author/artist that inspired one of the most challenging creative projects of my life. Some will no doubt ask me why, how Plath and I found each other on the page? The answer was in Jacqueline Rose's *The Haunting of Sylvia Plath,* "'*Not ghosts, exactly but presences,*' '*They're waiting,*' '*They come back* [...] reliving each past *event* [...] *vivid and irrevocable* [...] *and would continue to exist long after their own voices were stilled.*'" Sylvia, she still is in me. And I love the fact that she visited me and inspired this origin story and my tribute to her, the collection of cento poems you are holding in your hand.

So, it starts off last November in Whittier, CA. I was at a reading, book launch, for the horror poetry anthology *Dark Ink*, that included one of my own poems, published by Moon Tide Press. It was at this reading where I met one of my social media friend's poet LeAnne Hunt there. While we were talking, she mentioned a book of erasure poems called *Red* created from Bram Stoker's *Dracula*. Instantly, it this idea planted a seed. Cut to a few months later, I was going through a dark time. My Mami passed away in 2018 and the stress from this time caused me to get sick. I suffered back to back illnesses. Whopping Cough, colds, flu which led to dark depression. And during one of those times, I was sitting in my chair in a very dark place, in the office where I write in our apartment, and as I turned I saw this copy of *The Bell Jar* staring back at me from the bookshelf. I wanted to get my creative mind away from the stress, from the illness and just write.

So, I opened Plath's book and something inside me said, let's try something. This is when I went back to the conversation I had with Leanne about *Red* and Chase Berggrun's erasure poem take on Bram Stoker's *Dracula*. Like I said, I was sick and I wanted to distract and challenge myself trying to craft these cento poems. This was new to me. I was never successful with this poetry form before I began this project. Sylvia Plath once said, *"I want someone to mouth me."* And when I started this cento project that's what I did. From chapter one I just culled individual words from the chapter. I tried to stay away from pairs and just took single words and tried to craft a poem. The only thing I used was the first line as title for each chapter. My goal was to write 20 poems, for each chapter, and complete the project in twenty days. This creative experiment was such a challenge. It would take hours. After each poem, I would be drenched in sweat. After the 3rd of 5th chapter, I had the feeling like I was truly starting to connect with Plath and something magical was happening on each page I was crafting. Every day I was mesmerized going through each and every word Plath had selected for each page on every chapter of *The Bell Jar*. Seeing Sylvia's word choices was amazing and inspiring. The best thing was that the poems I was shaping kept getting better and better. And by the end, there was still this question mark and the voices of dread and doubt were hounding me as I kept asking, is this anything? Is this project any good?

The first person I showed was my wife. She is the Plath scholar of the family, *The Bell Jar* book on the shelf was hers, and since she has loved reading Sylvia her whole life, she would tell me if this project was working or not. Immediately after reading a few poems, her response was uplifting, supportive and my wife was fascinated with theses cento poems. Best of all, she thought it was a very unique idea. So, then I decided to show a few poets. I sent off my work-in-progress manuscript, I waited and waited and heard nothing but crickets. Then I messaged a poet I know who is familiar with my work. I sent her my manuscript and their response was critical but very honest. Still, my belief in this project never wavered. This is when I decided to write the Poet's note. I felt like this is what my project was missing for the reader to understand my intentions and how this project was made. After I added the note, I started sending *La Belle Ajar* to other poets and their response was more positive. The Poet's Note definitely helped and was one of the last pieces missing from my manuscripts. Soon after adding the Poet's Note is when I started submitting my manuscript to contests and publications. But the result was nothing but rejection, after rejection and more rejection. I remember I had suggested to my friend Amy Shimson-Santo that she should submit her poetry manuscript to CLASH Books. She did and a few weeks later, I was about to go to sleep and a voice, I like to think it was Sylvia, telling me to send my manuscript to CLASH Books and I did. Six days later, they loved *La Belle Ajar*, I signed the contract and the rest is history. It goes to show, always listen to that voice.

My creative voice has never steered me wrong, and it led me to Sylvia Plath.

Sivvy changed my life. She was there for me during my darkest times and her words and the words that I "mouthed" from her, crafted the book in your hands. And I am indebted to her inspiration. In fact, to honor Plath, I've invested every last dollar from our bank account in just about every Plath book, biography, literary criticism, that I could get my hands one. I feel like I've been going to Plath school since I finished this project and reading all of these books has been nothing but a joy. It's like I can still commune with Sylvia Plath. We hang out each night when I open one of these books, she is there with me. I am still learning from one of my all time favorite poet and writer and just like when I started this project, I am enjoying every word on the page. She saved me. And this collection of poems is my way of saying Thank You Sylvia for inspiring all these poems, *The Bell Jar* will always resonate within me.

RECOMMENDED READING

Below I have listed of books I read and devoured before, during and after the writing of *La Belle Ajar*. Going to Plath school and (re)learning about my favorite poet was one of the most enlightening and life changing reading experiences in my life as a reader, writer and a poet. I urge you to dive inside the pages of these amazing volumes on Sylvia Plath.

Essential:

The Bell Jar
Ariel: The Restored Edition
The Complete Poems
The Colossus and other poems
Johnny Panic and the Bible of Dreams
The Unabridged Journals of Sylvia Plath
Letters Home: Correspondence 1950-1963: Volume 1
The Letters of Sylvia Plath: Volume 2
Mary Ventura and the Ninth Kingdom

Literary Criticism, Critical Study and Analysis:

The Silent Woman by Janet Malcom
Malcolm goes behind the scene to chronicle the battle of the legacy of Plath between the Hughes family estate and the biographers and writers who want to bring Sylvia's life to light.

The Death and Life of Sylvia Plath by Ronald Hayman
The Observer said it best when they wrote: "An excellent new study, conscientious and well-balanced, with narrative conviction that keeps on reading tensely from Plath's death to birth and back..."

Sylvia Plath: A Critical Study by Tim Kendall
One of my favorite lit crit books on Plath, has fascinating insights into her writing, a must for all Plathian scholars and readers, alike.

The Haunting of Sylvia Plath by Jacqueline Rose

American Literature raved: "The Haunting of Sylvia Plath gives us a new Sylvia Plath... Rose's book, original deftly argued and bold... will render most exciting of Plath obsolete."

Poetic License: Essays on Modernist and Postmodernist Lyric by Marjorie Perloff
A must for all Plathians includes one of the best essays ever written about Sylvia's poetry: "The two Ariels: the (re)making of the Sylvia Plath canon."

The Art of Sylvia Plath: edited by Charles Newman
An extraordinary collection of essays that includes selections from A. Alvarez, Anne Sexton and Mary Ellman's most excellent piece "The Bell Jar—An American girlhood."

Sylvia Plath: The Woman & The Work: edited by Edward Butscher
A fantastic collection of essays that include such luminary Sylvia scholars such as Marjorie Perloff and Joyce Carol Oates.

Ariel Ascending: Writings About Sylvia Plath edited by Paul Alexander
Another stellar collection of essays that included celebrated Plathian scribes like A. Alvarez, Joyce Carol Oates, Anne Sexton and Sylvia's own mother Aurelia S. Plath.

Critical Insights: Sylvia Plath edited by William K. Buckley
The Unraveling Archive: Essays on Sylvia Plath edited by Anita Helle
Critical Insights: The Bell Jar edited by Janet McCann
The Bell Jar: A Novel of the Fifties: Linda Wagner-Martin
Great Writers Series: Sylvia Plath by Peter K. Steinberg
Sylvia Plath: A Literary Life: Linda Wagner-Martin

Biographies

There are so many biographies that I cannot choose one. Some books been authorized by the Plath estate, others are crafted without authorization. My advice is to read them all and decide for yourself.

Because of these some of these are favored
over others, I have listed the book in alpha-
betical order by author's last name

Rough Magic: A biography of Sylvia Plath
by Paul Alexander
Giving Up: The Last Days of Sylvia Plath
by Jillian Becker
Sylvia Plath: A Biography by Lindsay
Wagner Martin
*Her Husband: Hughes and Plath- A
Marriage* by Diane Middlebrook
*American Isis: The Life and Art of Sylvia
Plath* by Carl Rollyson
The Last Days of Sylvia Plath by Carl
Rollyson
Bitter Fame: A Life of Sylvia Plath by Anne
Stevenson

ACKNOWLEDGMENTS

Gracias to Amy Shimson-Santo, Leanne Hunt, Andrea Auten and Christina Strigas for your feedback on this project in its infant stages and early incarnations. Thank You to my lovely wife Michelle for believing in me by encouraging me and letting me know that this project was something that needed to be discovered and read by other writers and artists. This book would not be possible without the belief and support by Christoph Paul and Leza Cantoral. Thank You CLASH Books for publishing this project that helped me through a time that was one of the darkest in my life.

ABOUT THE AUTHOR

Photo by Rachel Warecki

Adrian Ernesto Cepeda is the author of the full-length poetry collection *Flashes & Verses... Becoming Attraction*s from Unsolicited Press, the poetry chapbook *So Many Flowers, So Little Time* from Red Mare Press, *Between the Spine* published with Picture Show Press. Adrian is an LA Poet who has a BA from the University of Texas at San Antonio and he is also a graduate of the MFA program at Antioch University in LA where he lives with his lovely wife.

TRAGEDY QUEENS: STORIES INSPIRED BY LANA DEL REY & SYLVIA PLATH

Edited by Leza Cantoral

CENOTE CITY

Monique Quintana

99 POEMS TO CURE WHATEVER'S WRONG WITH YOU OR CREATE THE PROBLEMS YOU NEED

Sam Pink

PAPI DOESN'T LOVE ME NO MORE

Anna Suarez

ARSENAL/SIN DOCUMENTOS

Francesco Levato

FOGHORN LEGHORN

Big Bruiser Dope Boy

WE PUT THE LIT IN LITERARY

CLASHBOOKS.COM

FOLLOW US

TWITTER

IG

FB

@clashbooks